BETWEEN SPIRIT & SUBSTANCE

THE SILENT VOICE OF LIFE

BY
DAVID STEWART HANDELMAN

Gotham Books

30 N Gould St.
Ste. 20820, Sheridan, WY 82801
https://gothambooksinc.com/
Phone: 1 (307) 464-7800

© 2023 David Stewart Handelman. All rights reserved.

No part of this book may be reproduced,
stored in a retrieval system, or transmitted by
any means without the written permission of the author.

Published by Gotham Books (February 4, 2023)

ISBN: 979-8-88775-196-2 (sc)
ISBN: 979-8-88775-197-9 (e)

Because of the dynamic nature of the Internet,
any web addresses or links contained in this book may
have changed since publication and may no longer be valid.

The views expressed in this work are solely those of
the author and do not necessarily reflect the views
of the publisher, and the publisher hereby disclaims
any responsibility for them.

CONTENT

Books by David Stewart Handelman	iii
Dedication	iv
Introduction	vi
Live a Life that Matters	- 1 -
Desert Winds	- 3 -
Lost Loves	- 4 -
Postcards	- 6 -
Oceans Away	- 7 -
Life Renewed	- 8 -
A New Pair of Glasses	- 9 -
Statues	- 11 -
Silent Morning	- 12 -
Rose Garden	- 13 -
Room for Rent	- 14 -
Mortality	- 15 -
Bands of Gold	- 16 -
Empty Chairs	- 17 -
The Picture Frame	- 18 -
Rain Drops	- 19 -
Ghosts	- 21 -
Silent Tears	- 22 -
The Willow Tree	- 24 -
Santa Fe	- 25 -
The Wedding Dress	- 27 -
The Party	- 28 -
Stardust	- 29 -
Drifting Away	- 30 -
Autumn	- 32 -
Time	- 33 -
Silent Memories	- 34 -
Heaven is Falling	- 35 -
Recovered Voices	- 36 -

The Cookbook	- 37 -
Payback	- 38 -
Bloodline	- 39 -
Reasons	- 40 -
Close Your Eyes	- 41 -
Naked	- 42 -
Try Me	- 43 -
Late Night Train	- 44 -
River's Edge	- 45 -
Our Checkbook	- 46 -
Walls	- 48 -
Masquerade	- 49 -
Three Hours Past Midnight	- 50 -
Letter to My Father	- 51 -
Face in the Clouds	- 52 -
Time Passed	- 53 -
The Train Ride	- 55 -
Index	- 61 -
About the Author	- 64 -

Books by

David Stewart Handelman:

"Never Lose a Commission Sale Again"
A guide for Real Estate Agents

"Sentiments"
A book of Prose, Poetry and Thoughts

"Notes from a Quill"
Parchment scratches to Soothe the Day

"Words in Rhythm"
Poems and thoughts to Open Your Heart

"Between Spirit & Substance"
The silent Voice of Life

"The Gravel Road" A Novel

"The Assassin's Wife" A Novel

Dedication

Judy

My Children, Alisa & Jeffrey

This book is of my thoughts, dreams, hopes, and experiences in my life which are far too numerous to mention.

I am in earnest hope that you, the reader, will enjoy my notes, scribbles and writings from my heart and lifelong travels, peeking into the heart of a lost soul.

Too often we underestimate the power of a touch, a smile, a kind word, a listening ear, an honest compliment, or the smallest act of caring, all of which have the potential to turn a life around.

--Leo Buscaglia (1924-1998)

Introduction

Each poem is a story that is told through the eyes, thoughts and mind of the person telling or writing the story. You, the reader, must determine your own value of each of those stories.

As you read this book, try to put yourself into the heart of each individual story as it relates to oneself.

By doing this, you can feel and imagine it, by putting yourself into the place where it was written about, where or what the author is trying to say.

By accomplishing this, you feel the passion, heart and soul of the author, and the story. At that point, fully enjoy the written words as it relates to you.

This is a new day.

This is the beginning of a new day.

God has given me this day to use as I will.

I can waste it or use it for good.

What I do today is important because

I am exchanging a day of my life for it.

When tomorrow comes, this day will be gone forever, leaving in its place something that I have traded for it.

I want it to be gain, not loss; good not evil; success not failure; in order that I shall not regret the price that I paid for it.

                -- David Stewart Handelman

Live a Life that Matters

Ready or not, someday it will all come to an end

There will be no more sunrises or sunsets, no seconds, minutes, hours, or days.

All the things that you collected, whether they be treasures or baubles, will surely pass to someone else.

Your wealth, fame and temporal power will shrivel to irrelevance.

It will not matter what you owned or what you were owed.

Your grudges, resentments, frustrations and jealousies will finally disappear.

So too, your hopes, ambitions, plans and to-do lists will cease and expire.

The wins and losses that once seemed so important, will fade away.

It won't matter where you came from, or what side of the tracks you lived on at the end.

It won't matter whether you were beautiful or brilliant.

Even your gender and skin color will be irrelevant.

So, what will matter? How will the value of your days be measured?

What will matter is not what you bought, but what you built; not what you got, but what you gave.

What will matter is not your success, but your significance.

What will matter, is not what you have learned, but what you have taught.

What will matter is every act of integrity, compassion, or sacrifice that enriched, empowered or encouraged others to emulate your example.

What will matter is not your competence, but your character.

What will matter is not how many people you knew, but how many people will feel a lasting loss when you're gone.

What will matter is not your memories, but the memories that live in those that loved you.

What will matter is how long you will be remembered, by whom and for what.

Living a life that matters, does not happen by accident. It's not a matter of circumstance, but of choice.

-- *David Stewart Handelman*

Desert Winds

Desert winds,
Blowing, glowing golden sands,
Of time passed,
Always going,
Ever shifting and ever flowing.

The dry seas,
Moon shining, glowing in the night,
The sun rising high,
Light winds blowing,
Gleaming in the bright, early in the morning light.

We are but a grain of sand,
In the deserts of the world,
A world so hurled,
Moving with the winds and sands,
A world so twirled.
As we travel,
Decisions we make,
Turning, changing, moving,
Always moving, moving.

With the timelessness of the sands,
Crossing, blowing,
Over the many open vast lands.
Do something special,
Think through your actions,
Our life is full of transactions.

Be kind to another as we
Blow across the land,
After all we are, but a grain of sand.

Lost Loves

Traveling along,
I've lost so much,
My life and loves,
Gone forever,
Never again to feel or touch.

They came in and out the door,
Around the world,
Travels galore,
Lost loves have gone forever more.

The women I loved,
The women I've lost,
Some I miss, some not,
And some I long to touch.

Loneliness I feel,
No one to hold,
Only a blanket tucked neatly in my bed fold.
Days have gone by
And time marches on,
I remember most,
My life's plays
As I butter my toast.

Never married,
Couldn't find the right one,
As I look back,
I see what I've missed and miss what I see,
No one left to love me.

When the trees sing, it doesn't really matter if you know the song, or if you know the words, or even if you know the tune. What really matters, is knowing that the trees are singing at all.

--Mattie Stepanek

Postcards

Cards with pictures,
From near and far,
Little notes,
I miss you,
Having fun,
Went here and there,
I went to a fun fair.

Flying high,
The world around,
The swap meet was grand,
Everything was at our beckoned command.

The cards came, miss you more,
The card would say.
Can't wait to see you,
Be home soon,
Perhaps maybe, just maybe sometime in June.

Days and months turn into years,
Only a postcard,
Now receiving less,
The cards say, "God bless."
Nothing now,
The cards cease to come.
I know you're busy,
Too much to do,
Oh yeah,
I miss you too.

Oceans Away

Waiting, waiting,
Together we were,
Letters you send to me,
Longing to be together and free.

We write each other,
Love poems and sonnets,
Write about what was,
The flights of the beautiful white doves.
When will you come home to me?
Years have passed,
Is our love going to last?

I miss you more each day,
You are so far away,
Storms brewing,
The oceans rough at times,
When the bells toll,
Will you be mine?
Years passed
And time flows slowly,
The last letter you said,
It's been too long,
Find someone new to play your song.

I am too far, and I have someone new,
I'm not returning home,
The ocean waters cold,
Now, waters have turned to foam.

Life Renewed

It was dark and rainy,
Early in the morn,
A baby cries, just born.

Parents gleeful at the sight,
To see new life and all its might.
A new generation born to be,
To carry on tradition and someday a new family.

Down the hall as people wept,
A man of years has gone from light,
No more to be in sight.
He was a good man,
Lonely and sad,
I miss him so,
He was my dad.

After a long life
And a good fight,
His plane has left on its last flight.

An adventure of life he did pass,
Of trial and work
A family he did build,
To the lives, he left filled.

Never to be forgotten,
His life will be missed,
Decisions he made and remembered for his life's journey,
His body rolling down the hall on a gurney.

A New Pair of Glasses

We see different things
As we stare out into space,
Some people look in
And others look out,
Be careful of the ones,
That wants to scream and shout.

The color of roses,
All pinkish, red, white and bright,
Makes us some time act foolish,
Some waiting for a fight and others waits for a flight.

Each one sees a different world,
Through different colored glasses,
Watching people move fast
And others move like molasses.
Put on the glasses that show what it is,
See all that is truth,
The real that we stare,
At all that is out there.

Look and see what reality is,
The truth, honesty at best,
Be true to yourself,
Do not look away,
Don't put it on the shelf.

Only wear the glasses that are clear,
See the world for what it is,
You cannot hide,
Do not brush aside,
Look at all the colors,
From afar and wide.

*When you fall in life, it does not matter
what you fall upon or where you fall,
What matters is how quickly you get up.*

--David Stewart Handelman

Statues

They stand in all their glory,
Cold and lonely,
Plaster, marble, Onyx, or concrete,
The life lived in the past,
In awe, we stare,
Of the statues that stand so boldly there.

What kind of life did they portray?
Were they worthy of the mixture or clay?
Was it something of beauty?
Deeds or work, or did they betray?

Past in antiquity,
For all to share,
For all to glare,
Look hard,
They will not scare.
Do we know the truth about the statue standing there?

Some of beauty,
Others of glory,

There they are,
The past, behold,
Standing,
To show everyone who they were,
Standing alone in the winter's cold.

Silent Morning

Gazing across the meadows,
From high on the knoll,
Into the early morning hazy mist,
Through the passes,
Down into the valleys,
Not to be missed.

The glow of the slight light rising,
Every new day is surprising as the sun's glow is sizing.

Rising to welcome the day,
All the majesty,
On this sun filled, brightly lit Sunday.

This is the gift,
Look all around, Look,
Beauty, like a plentiful buffet.

I never dreamed I would see so clearly,
I hear the songbirds loudly praising the day.

Hold my hand, tenderly,
As we walk through the early morning mist,
On the soft, gentle grassy mound.

Feel the fresh moisture on our bare feet.
Grass gliding through our toes.
Each blade tickles,
How funny it feels,
Such a strange feeling,
An experience such as this,
Early, in the morning's mist.

Rose Garden

Strolling down the rugged stone and pebbled path,
Reminds me of life past,
Smell the flowers,
The Roses sweetest of all,
Walking slowly, almost to a crawl.

The air filled with sweet scents,
Jasmine crawling high on the vines,
Their aroma filling the air,
Like someone cooking,
With beautiful perfumes as the sweet scents,
Fill my world.

I cannot imagine life without the simple things,
A look,
A smile,
A simple touch,
The slight smell of the rose bush soothing,
Filling the air,
In this world,
Not a care.

Beauty abounds,
Everywhere you look,
The sun,
The stars,
The moon's glow is so bright.

Peace all around,
There is nothing to scare,
No harm can come to you,
Not in this place tonight.

Room for Rent

The bed, chest,
The bookcase so tall,
The tilted picture hanging on the wall.
This was the room at the end of the hall,
The music box playing,
The dim light glimmers,
Through the light, dusty tasseled shade.
The room painted blue, for all the tears I shed for you.

I feel your touch,
Remembering your arms tightly wrapped around my body,
Sliding, crossing my bare chest.
Your head against my back,
Your golden hair flowing across my body,
Touching, holding.
Your light, warm, tender kisses,
Your breath of desire upon my body,
Holding as you pressed against me surrounding my soul.
                Empty
                     Gone
                           Lonely now
Only the music box softly playing,

Memories of lives past, there was no clue that it would not last.
My memories burning forever will live here.

Now empty,

                ROOM FOR RENT

Mortality

Sometimes I question my mortality and wonder if anyone will remember me when I have passed on.

Will anyone give my existence a second thought that I had lived or existed at all?

There are so many unanswered questions that I have about life in general, I sustain periods or times that I get very overwhelmed.

Did I do anything that will make an impact on anyone else in their life?

Am I going to be remembered for an evil deed or the saving of one's life, either body or soul?

Was I a good and true friend?

Will I be remembered for charity?

Will my children or grandchildren remember me?

Will I leave fond memories, or am I to die in obscurity?

The real measure of a person's wealth is how much you'd be worth if you lost all your money.

Will I have the time see all the beauty that the world has to offer?

As we travel down our life's road and cross the many lands, a person's life can either be cultivated, or allow ourselves to turn the fruit of life into a desert of sand and weeds without hearing the sounds and the sweet, gentle calling of the birds.

As I age, and my time is fleeting by,

I will never cease to question and wonder,

The magical, mystical, simple word, "Why."

Bands of Gold

Precious metals will bind,
Holding tightly around the finger,
This is what we show to all,
A visual clue to let the world know.

It's not the metal that will shine,
The sounds of the heart,
And with these rings,
We will not depart.

Rings do not hold
Two people together,
Only the heart to be told,
Without the love, there is nothing to behold.

The rings tell the world
Of what we are,
Married to each other,
Look not for another.

Tell each other of devotion,
Do not let it slip by,
There are rules that apply,
These rules you cannot buy.

A taste of life's drink,
Is not always filled with a magic potion,
Nor is it a soothing lotion.

The bands of gold do not bind the heart,
Only metal to show,
Never hide feelings in a booth,
Your heart tells the truth.

Empty Chairs

The large room at the banquet hall,
With many seats to fill,
Who will be seated?
Will it be of their free will?

The chairs remain empty,
In the room, so cold,
So, large,
It is something to behold.

The lights flicker,
In this room, so old,
People waiting, standing in line to collect the gold.

Hard work will prevail,
To those who avail,
Given a chair,
Sit if you dare.

Don't be nervous,
Or fear the unknown,
The music suddenly will stop,
A chair, waiting for you alone.

Life takes us around the chairs,
As the music plays loudly,
When it comes to a stop,
Pay attention,
This is not a life swap.

The Picture Frame

Who shall fit in the picture frame?
Only the one that left the mark,
Generous at best,
Did they pass the big test?

Brothers, sisters, cousins, and all,
Daughters and sons,
Don't forget Mom and Dad,
Old family and even the ones
That went mad.

Our childhood and graduation,
Weddings the best,
Everybody moving to the still,
Travel pictures and more,
See all the rest,
This is not a screen test.

The boat and the house,
Look who is standing in front,
For all to see,
Look again at you and me.

Is this what it is?
Or is it something that we did,
Are we so proud that we must portray?
Our good deeds,
In the picture frame on display.

Rain Drops

The dark clouds of gray and black,
The winds blow,
Fast and cold,
Flowing quickly down the hills,
So, fast, it gives me the chills.

Light the fireplace,
Put in the logs,
Now darker outside,
Here come the dogs.
Slight trickle of wet,
Landing on the windows,
Wind sounds louder through the door,
Is this the calm before the roar?

The trickle of the wet lightly tapping the window,
The roar of the noise as the thunder bangs loudly in the sky.

Rain stronger, smashing the roof tiles like balls of fury being thrown by the Gods.
 The clouds in rage, anger, and fury.

A Game by them as they laugh with glee,
They say let's play a game for thee.
The grounds get covered, wheat crops, grassy mounds of earth, covered as oceans gain strength in height as it fills with the loud down pour of water from the skies.

The Gods laugh as they watch the things of earth scurry,
Watch them run as if they are in a hurry.

The skies clear as the sun gleams through the trees,
Slight winds shake and quiver the leaves.
The new day begins, again, everybody wins.

Ghosts

By accident it happened,
What did I do?
I didn't think, there was no chance to blink.

Don't open the door,
Kept it closed for all time,
Splitting at the seams,
Quick, grab the locks,
I could not stand it anymore,
Everything stuffed tightly into a drawer.

Kept closed during my time,
Storing the hurt and pain,
Disappointments and rejections,
Silent fears and tears,
It fills my closet of many, many years.

It was so full I tried to lock,
But I could not block,
The doors swing open,
The noises in my head,
All my ghosts of past I dread.

Now time has passed, and my life changed.
Occasionally,
I pass the door,
Put on an extra lock,
That shall remain closed for ever more.

I'll never tell, and no one will know,
Who am I?
This person that stands here aglow happy and smiles,
The door will be buried at last,
Hiding all my ghosts' past.

Silent Tears

It was late night, or was it in the dark, black, early morning.
The streetlights flickering through the shade.

He slowly rises from once again, another endless, sleepless night, being careful not to disturb his wife sleeping next to him.

He walks slowly into a separate room in the far end house where he seeks quiet solace.

A quiet place, a room separate from the rest of the world where he can be alone. Quietly, the door closes behind him with the sound of the latch engaging.

His thoughts take him into a sadness that he can no longer bear.
One at a time, each eye, tears slowly roll down his cheeks.

Trying to be brave, holding back something that he has no control of.

Suddenly it happens; he can no longer hold the sadness that has built up throughout the many years.

So, strong he was during his life, brave to all, no fear from anything.
Always open arms to hold the sad and sorrow. Give faith to those that had none.

The time has come, the man breaks with the pent-up sorrow of his own personal world.

The tears quietly start flowing like rain in a wild storm.

No longer can he hold the world within, thinking he was brave and courageous.

On this night, his time has come. His world has come apart, crushing down on him.

Sadness, broken heart, pent up anger and sorrow that he can no longer bear on this night, this very special night,

He cries uncontrollably the tears of the many, many years.

The dawn breaks as he slowly opens the door to return to the life that nobody knew to be strong and consoling to those in need.

He is again, brave.

The Willow Tree

The branches Weep,
Looking so sad,
Rising so high in all its glory,
Each branch has its own story.

It stands so tall,
Crying all the time,
The green color,
Gives life a new name,
No one to blame.

Why so sad the tree standing there,
Lonely as it dominates its own place,
Standing, holding its own,
Growing to reach the top,
Sitting, growing on its own throne.

Roots buried so deep,
Why do people tear, cut and destroy?
The years of growth,
They think it is so grand,
All for the greed of the land.

It is no wonder,
That the tree willow,
Cries all the time.

People try to steal their thunder,
Sadness the tree cries.
As the Willow Tree,
Is cut down, down, falling to its demise.

Santa Fe

Traveling as fast as I can,
Across the country,
I run to you, I run to you.
I love you so much,
Don't know what to do.

I will find you,
Through growing cactus flowers wild,
In the garden, you wait,
I'm so nervous,
It is hard to contemplate.

I imagine you,
With a small flower in your hair,
Your dress flowing in the midnight air.

Miles to go,
My heart beating faster,
The black asphalt road flowing,
Empty the ground, moving, growing.

Closer, closer I come,
Looking for you,
In the morning sun,
Going home where I begun.

You are there,
I see you closer,
Walking in the garden,
The flowers, desert bloom,
Our life together will resume.

Together again,
We will meet in the city of Santa Fe.

The bitterness of poor quality long remains after the sweetness of low price is forgotten!

--David Stewart Handelman

The Wedding Dress

Searching through the storage all morning,
Mom finds the magic dress,
The one that she wore,
That changed her life that special day,
Now Mom and Dad,
We are going to give her away.

Now the time has come,
Her daughter has grown,
Now was her chance,
Her daughter's wedding dance.

She found her love,
She tried on the white glove.

"Look Mom, it fits,"
She said with a shout,
"Will I be happy like you?"
Mom said, "I have no doubt."

The special day arrived,
Her love to be,
"We have a lot to do, don't you agree?"

"I love you so," he said,
"My wife forever after,
You are beautiful in that dress,"
As the Judge says, "I bless."

"Mom, can I keep the dress for my child to see?"
"Someday she will wear on her special day,
When she finds her love and holds her beautiful bouquet."

The Party

Once a year,
The parties we had,
Everyone enjoyed,
Laughter was employed.

More and more came,
To the house, you see,
Bring food to share,
Listen to the musical fare.

A few were jealous,
They wanted their own,
To take away,
To have their own party,
They wanted their own buffet.

Time passed,
Moved by the years,
What they did,
Took laughter
And turned it into tears.

Now parties are no more,
Happiness and laughter,
Put into a drawer.

The holiday is silent,
Their jealous behavior,
Destroyed it for all,
Now with a few friends,
We go to the movies at the mall.

Stardust

Pockets full of magical dust,
Sprinkle here and there,
Keep the children from fear and scare.
Sprinkle the dust
All around their room,
Fairies arrive fluttering gaily around their sleepy heads.

Giving dreams of clowns and toys,
All good things,
Some quiet, most without noise.

The dust of magic,
For all little girls and boys,
Far and wide,
Get on the magic pony,
Come, don't hesitate,
Let's take a ride.

Around we go,
The sprinkle of magic more,
Believe in magic,
Close your eyes,
Close your eyes,
Dreams and wishes would come true,
As you dream,
Remember, I love you.

Drifting Away

Just you and me,
From the start,
We were lovers,
Everyone could see,
We were now one,
Just you and me.

Married for life,
Our hearts would meld,
So, the story would be told,
Our life together was gold.

I thought it would last forever,
Through all kinds of weather,
No matter what,
We held together like leather.

Time passed
And we cared for each other,
Time moved so quickly,
We tried each to smother.

Thoughts changed,
And so, did our lives,
Words thrown like knives.

No more dreams to share,
We cannot talk,
Anger withheld,
No speaking when we walk.

We slowly drifted away in silence,
Without words spoken,
Love diminished,
Our lives together, finished.

Going from us,
To you and me,
What would life bring?
Was this just a fling?

The only thing left,
Silent words echoing in the hollow,
In tears, so hard to swallow.

Gone are the days of joy and laughter,
The days of old,
I thought would last forever.

Everything dismissed.

I guess in life nothing lasts,
The stones that were thrown,
Given in spite and hate,
Are now stones cast.

Our lives together now gone,
Now buried deep in the past,
I thought that it was good,
Sometimes,
I shed tears that it did not last.

Autumn

I can't wait for the turn,
Autumn colors along the road,
A slight wind chills with a breeze,
All the colors of the rainbow
And gentle pleasant, perfumed aromas fill the air.

Green, orange, yellow and more,
The turn on the country byways, back roads, and highways,
As the wind blows through my hair,
More colors everywhere.

I cannot imagine more colors anywhere,
Like crayons coloring the trees and the sky,
Never ending beauty all around,
Stop the cart, look again,
I take a deep breath, I sigh.

A slight cool chill in the air surrounds me as I stand on the slight dirt hilly mound looking across the valley at the wheat blowing, weaving in and out and swaying as if it were dancing to the music of the gods.

This is the autumn found in my dreams waiting for the movement of the wheeled horse drawn cart to carry me to market.

The day will come again when I see the beautiful colors on the rolling hillsides, hand painted artistry by the angels.

These are moments in time,
The paintbrush of the Gods,

                          Autumn

Time

As the clock ticks,
The numbers remain the same,
The hands move past,
Time moving so fast.
Things to do,
Run fast,
Go here, go there,
Do not miss,
Even by a hair.
Do not stop,

Beat the clock,
Everybody moves so fast.
So quickly they stumble,
If not careful,
They will tumble.
Take the time
To smell something sweet,
Slow down, live,
Look to the stars,
Our lives must survive.
Do not stare at the clock,
You must move,
Our time is short,
Seek, explore, live,
Make a note in life,
Do something with yourself,
Before we must report.

Silent Memories

Sitting alone in the rocking chair,
Looking out into space,
I cannot help myself but to see all my memories before me.

No one to share,
The stories that I hold,
Some were bad
And some were gold.

The people that I loved,
The people that I knew,
Some laughed and some were blue.

Friends now gone,
No more enemies,
I've outlived them all,
Only the children are left,
Once a month,
They give me a call.

If I'm lucky,
They take me to the mall.

I miss the old days,
They were carefree and loose,

Some short and some tall.
Now there is nothing to hide,
Those days are gone,
My memories are all that I have left,

Heaven is Falling

The sky is falling
Clouds clinging to nothing
Rainbows rapidly changing colors
Rising and fading out of sight.

The sky rains fall heavily filling the waters,
The sky clears but for a moment, just to tease us.

Mountains crashing against each other with a push of the whirl winds.

The vast oceans rising as high as the eye can see,
Heaven is falling,
The sky is falling.

The rage of the earth retaliating from years, centuries of abuse.

Rape the ground and the earth's body of our very existence!!!!
Rape the trees and oceans.
Stop!!! STOP!!!!!! STOP!!!!!!

The ravaging abuse must stop if we are to continue.

Live free,

                Breathe

Recovered Voices

Staying silent for years,
I sit and stare into space,
There were fun times for me,
And some voices in disgrace.

Bring back the laughter,
Smiles and glee,
Rise the joys for all to see.

Come join us,
Do not wait,
Not only in the days of May,
But now and after,

Every day do not delay.

Recovering sounds and voices I long to hear,
Noises from far and near,
Missing are the sounds that I miss,
Birds chirping, trees flowing,
High winds lightly blowing.

The rustling of the leaves,
The sounds of the shifting sands in the wind,
Words and sounds from yesterday,
The roads of the world so defined.

I hear, I listen,
Shush, be quiet and still,
Listen to the miracles of sound,
Some loud and some profound,
Remember this,
We only have one go around.

The Cookbook

Follow the recipe,
Get the ingredients,
Put them on the table,
Check the label.

Pour it in the bowl,
Blend it light,
Use the large spoon
And stir with all your might.

Stir, mix, and add for the blend,
Ingredients seem to never end,
If things are to bake well,
Listen for the sound of the oven's bell.

Stir more and blend,
Add sugar to the rest,
This is not a test.

The oven temperature's hot,
Ready for the dish,
Thirty-five beats with the wooden spoon,
Get the spatula to scrape the bowl,
Grease the pan and pour this is fun and not a chore.

Waiting for the time,
As the oven lights the dish,
Starting to bubble,
Hope the dish isn't in trouble.

Finally, the finish and ready to eat,
This is dinner,
I followed the book, and I am now the cook.

Payback

A gift in passing,
I gave to them,
Just a kind gift, I thought,
For something that could not be bought.

I felt sorry for them,
Standing in the cold shivering in the wind,
They took my gift and grinned.

A smile of thank you from deep in their heart,
"I will not forget you," was the remark.

Time passed and two years later,
I passed the corner only to see,
A man passing out change to another who was in need.

He looked up at me and saw something as he walked over to where I was standing.
"I did not forget your good deed," he said.
"Your gift brought me back to reality.

Your kindness given from your heart was all I needed.
You helped me when I was down and brought me back to life.
Turning a person's life into a picture painted with a palette knife."

"Now it is my turn to give back from your good deed."

It is now my moment to give someone courage as you had given me.
Maybe someday they will also give to a person in need,
A gift, payback if you will,
Is found in a simple, single dollar bill.

Bloodline

Plant the seeds,
Mixed with an egg,
New life forms,
Be ready for life's storms.

Follow the path of the family,
Does the deed that they see?
Blinded by their own,
They only want you to be.

Seek out your own destiny if you will,
Make your own life's glory,
Follow your path to your life's journey,
Make the decision without the attorney.

Don't let the past destroy what you have,
Live for today,
Seek tomorrow the challenges of the day,
Whatever you do,
Do not spend your time playing croquet.

Follow the drumbeat,
You hear from your own echoes,
Do not follow the geckos,
They have no place to go.

Learn what you can,
Make you path grow wider,
Learn from others,
Listen to the beat,
This is your life,
Whatever you do to yourself, do not cheat.

Reasons

I do not need a reason to love you,
There are too many,
I do not need a reason to care,
I do not need a reason to hold you,
I do not need a reason to call you on cue.

I cannot explain,
How I feel about you,
What is the hold that you have on me?

I question why you ask,
"Do you love me?"
"Of course, I do; can't you see?"

Through thick and thin,
The ups and downs,
We hang in there together,
No matter how many frowns.

Do I need any reasons to look at you?
Smile at you sleeping,
Knowing that I do not, or ever
Need a reason to love you.

Do I need a reason?
Love, accept,
Relish in the thought that love does not need a reason or excuse,
There is no chart to follow the feelings of the heart.

Close Your Eyes

Things happen
In the bright of the day,
Close your eyes,
Think, feel the sun bright,
Stand still,
Do not run.

Hold your head high, as the warmth penetrates your body,
Absorb the heat of the sun,
Life this day has just begun.

Nothing to fear,
Do not shed a tear,
Think of things to come and enjoy the summer sun.

Feel the warmth, the glow,
Of the mid day's heat,
Stare silently into the upper space,
A small hum or whisper is now in place.

Just imagine the pureness of the sky,
One cloud appearing, floating,
Slightly graying,
The rain yet to come,
Moving like it is playing.

This is what happens when you see what there is,
Imagination and wonders,
You can see the beauty of the day.

Close your eyes and dream,
Look for beauty all around,
Beauty served on a bouquet.

Naked

I stand there,
Alone, naked and bare,
My soul open,
Nothing to hide,
Only truth, nothing lied.

No more can I shield,
Life cannot be taken in stride.

Circles of the clock moving faster,
Bare and alone,
Here I stand,
Not forever after.

What did I do that causes you to stare?
As I stand here naked and bare?
My soul opens for you to see,
Am I all alone, just me?

Do you see what's inside of me?
Do you read my mind?
Am I cruel or kind?

Nothing to hide,
Everything open,
Naked, bare,
Getting ready to yell and shout.

Emotions rising,
Anger I feel,
I cry, I scream, I shout,
Please, please, let me be free,
Show me the way out.

Try Me

Push here and there,
The buttons if you will,
Will I work with the coin?
Am I a club to join?

Test the movement,
Turn the knob,
Flip the switch,
If I don't work,
Do not ditch.

Try something new
And maybe it will work,
If not,
Give it a shake or jerk.

Plug it in,
Turn the handle,
Not working?
Try again.

Give it a kick,
Push if you will,
Do not knock it over,
Not working,
Get the hammer and the drill as well.

Push, kick and try again,
Look movement,
It is working, it's working,
What a thrill,
Turn on the flame,
I now have a Bar-B-Q grill.

Late Night Train

Clickity clack, Clickity clack,
Over the lonely railroad track,
Breaking the evening still,
The steam rising,
In the late-night chill.

What do the boxcars hold?
Rambling across the country,
The train whistles blow,
The train comes your way,
The passing of another day.

Loose Gravel lay between the tie tracks,
Rising on the rail car's bottom.

The black shiny rails,
Noise of the rail splits,
Each piece of steel just fits.

I ride the rails,
To a land unknown,
I have got to run,
Nowhere to go,
I just follow the sun,
Until the day is done.

The time will come when I have a new home,
Find a family that I can call my own.

The train roars further into the black night, flowing,
The sun rising in the morn,
I am on my way to face the sun's glowing,
Someday, I will find out where I'm going.

River's Edge

Sitting on the shore,
The soft grass and still rolling, flowing moss,
Starring from the edge,
The waters rapidly flowing past,
Staring, unknowing if it is to last.

Slight ripples on the shore,
As the creek waters move by,
Over submerged pebbles and rocks,
Nothing in sight,
Not even boat docks.

The fish running with the flow,
Some jumping and some do not know.
This is where I want to be,
Loose, loving, at peace,
To be left alone on this day,
To be free,
Watching the flight of the Bumble Bee.

Consumed with the calm of the day,
Close my eyes,
Feel the warm glow of the summer heat,
I feel that my life is now complete.

Sitting on the river's edge,
On a bright summer's day,
No worries, no cares,
Out here, there are no musical chairs.

Our Checkbook

Born with a book full of checks and cash,
As we grow older, spend what we have,
As our life savings slowly dwindle with time.

When we run out,
Is this the end?

Make your life count,
As if nothing else matters.

Make a note,
Follow your path,
Do not spend all your birth given cash.

Replace you funds with doing good for all,
Fill your account with caring and love,
Make sure that it fits like a glove.

Do not defray your life as if it does not matter,
If you think you are going broke,
Go back to the latter.

Gather more cash,
As you travel through time,
Do not let your life not count,
It is never too late to recapitulate.

Motto to live by

Life should NOT be a journey to the grave with the intention of arriving safely in an attractive and well-preserved body, but rather to skid in sideways, body thoroughly used up, totally worn out, screaming, "WOO HOO, what a ride."

~ Rodger L. Hann

Walls

Driving down the open highways,
Open space as far as the eye can see,
The walls quickly closing in on me.

Everywhere you look,
Asphalt down below rolling beneath my wheels,
Running, running so fast,
I cannot outrun my past.

The walls of my past closing in on me,
Tighter than a person can stand,
Hearing echoes so loud,
My ears shake with the sound.

Open roads abound,
Long emptiness ahead,
Yelling, screaming so loud,
I cannot hear a sound.

Clogged with memories of long gone,
Attacking me from all sides,
Cannot run any faster,
Long roads again,
Rolling, rolling faster with no end in sight.

Where can I go to hide?
Walls closing in on me,
Only open roads to show,
Cannot run or hide,
I have nowhere to go.

Masquerade

The music plays,
All the masks aglow,
Welcome to the party,
Have a drink,
Laugh and be hearty.

Look at the costumes,
All bright and aglow,
Hold tight,
Do not let go.

Have a drink, two more,
Smile, be happy,
Laugh at the jokes,
Watch the folks.

No one knows what hides behind the masks and glow?
The laughs hidden,
Things and thoughts that were afraid to show.

Be happy and cheerful,
Keep back the tears and memories,
Of long gone, many years.

Live for today,
The parties just started,
Be happy again.

Whatever you do not show the hidden fears,
That we have maintained.
For Life is a ball,
There it is, look,
The party is just down the hall.

Three Hours Past Midnight

Since midnight,
The time moves as the hands roll slowly around the numbers
Skillfully placed on the rounded white and black dial.
One hour, the time runs so slowly,
Watching, moving, and waiting for you.

The second hour, again, waiting, watching, where are you?
Are you coming?
Time running, moving so slowly. Hurry, we must leave.
Swiftly, we must go quickly.
I think that I have waited for you forever and this moment.

Minutes moving,
Time slowing as the pointer on the wheel,
The time piece hanging on the wall.
Where are you, I must leave, get away, we can fly to the moon.

Approaching the magical hour as the second hand moves the minutes to our time.
Now, I see you, slowly walking, starting to run to me.
Rolling along the preset path you are only allowed to follow.

Waiting no more, my beautiful love had arrived. The time has come.
You are here for me.
The clock stops, now, the hands of the wheel seem to float in the air.
Watching, waiting no more.
Looking at my watch one more time,
My life has just begun, it's only
Three hours past midnight.

Letter to My Father

What do I say,
The paper I stare,
Where do I start?
What do I do?
The more I think,
Do I have enough ink?

So many questions to ask,
Why did it happen?
Where did you go?
You left me to the winds' blow.

You traveled so much,
Never home for long,
The conversations we never had, I miss,
Nothing was there,
Not even a kiss.

You were always gone
And that is a shame,
You missed out on many things,
All the happiness that life brings.

I grew up, thanks to my Mom,
Always looking for you,
Not even calls to see if I am standing or about to fall.

You went away
As you always have,
When your travels are done,
You returned expecting a family,
And there was none.

Face in the Clouds

The clouds rolling in,
Dark gray in color,
Lines and heights vary,
Heavy raindrops they carry.

Starting slightly,
The balance to follow,
Heavy to come,
Washing away,
The ground to become.

Staring up into the heavy, clouded day,
Looking at the clouds,
The winds looking foul,
The old man begins to growl.

Loud noises begin to happen,
The bulb shines brightly,
Intermittent hits light the sky,
The face in the clouds begins to cry.

What I see is a man with a beard,
The look on his face is to be feared.

So large is the face,
I am remembering the look.

When I was a child,
As I huddle under the bed quilt,
Nightmares to behold,
Tucked tightly in the bed,
Under the blanket fold.

Time Passed

We were in love years ago,
Time passed,
Off to college we went,
We were so content.

Time moved on,
And so, did we,
Lives of our own,
No letters,
No phone.

Years later,
In the grocery store,
You were there with child in your care.

We talked for hours,
About our life past,
You have a family,
And I have my career at last.

The dark clouds graying,
Snowing lightly outside,
"Gotta go," she said,
Sometimes, we hold on by a thread.

As a tear on her face started to slide,
We touched again,
And gave each other a tight hug.

I watched, frozen in the ground as she drove away,
I could not move,
My legs felt like clay.

Matured youth is a coalescence of mind and body that integrates the wonder and excitement of life with the wisdom of one's years.

~ Richard N. Rice
November 1989

Printed with permission from the author

The Train Ride

A while back, I read a remarkably interesting book that compared life to a Train Ride or a series of Train Rides.

Life is like a train ride, it read. We get on. We ride. We get off. We get back on and ride
some more.

There are accidents and there are delays.
At certain stops, there are surprises.
Some of these will translate into great moments of joy and some will result in profound sorrow.

When we are born and we first board the train, we meet people who we think will be with us for the entire journey.

These people are our parents.

Sadly, this is far from the truth. Our parents are with us for as long as we absolutely need them.

They too have journeys that they must complete.
We live on with the memories of their love, affection, friendship, guidance and their ever presence.

There are others who board the train and who eventually become particularly important to us in turn.

These people are our brothers, sisters, friends, and acquaintances, whom we will learn to love and cherish.
Some people consider their journey like a jaunty tour.
They will just go merrily along.

Others will encounter many upsets, tears, and losses on their journey. Others still, will linger on to offer a helping hand to anyone in need.
Some people on the train will leave an everlasting impression when they get off.
Some will get on and off the train so quickly, they will scarcely leave a sign that they ever traveled along with you or ever crossed your path.

We will sometimes be upset that some passengers, whom we love, will choose to sit in another compartment and leave us to travel on our own.

Then again, there is nothing that says we cannot seek them out anyway.

Nevertheless, once sought out and found, we may not even be able to sit next to them because that seat will already be taken.

That is okay……Everyone's journey will be filled with hopes, dreams challenges, setbacks, and goodbyes.
We must strive to make the best of it….no matter what.

We must constantly strive to understand our travel companions and look for the best in everyone.

Remember that at any moment during our journey, any one of our travel companions can have a weak moment and be in need or our help.

We too may hesitate or even trip.
Hopefully, we can count on someone being there to be supportive and understanding.

The bigger mystery of our journey is that we do not know when our last stop will come.

Neither do we know when our travel companions will make their last stop.

Not even those sitting in the seat next to us.
Personally, I know I will be sad to make my final stop....
I am sure of it.

My separation from all those friends and acquaintances I made during the train ride
will be painful. Leaving all those I'm closed to will be a sad thing....
But then again, I am certain that one day I'll get to the main station only to meet up with everyone else.

They will all be carrying their baggage.... Most of which they did not have when they first got on the train.

I will be glad to see them again.

I will also be glad to have contributed to their baggage and to have enriched their lives, just as much as they will have contributed to my baggage and enriched my life.

We are all on this train ride together.

Above all, we should all try to strive to make the ride as pleasant and memorable as we can, right up until we each make the final stop and leave the train for the last time.

Index

A
Autumn   32

B
Bands of Gold   16
Bloodline   39

C
Close Your Eyes   41
Cookbook   37

D
Desert Winds   3
Drifting Away   30

E
Empty Chairs   17

F
Face in the Clouds   52

G
Ghosts   21

H
Heaven is Falling   35

I
J
K

L
Late Night Train   44
Letter to My Father   51
Life Renewed   8
Live a Life that Matters   1

Lost Loves   4

M
Masquerade   49
Mortality   15

N
Naked   42
New Pair of Glasses   9

O
Ocean's Away   7
Our Checkbook   46

P
Party   28, 49
Payback   38
Picture Frame   18
Postcards   6

Q

R
Rain Drops   19
Reasons   40
Recovered Voices   36
Room for Rent   14
Rose Garden   13

S
Santa Fe   25
Silent Memories   34
Silent Morning   12
Silent Tears   22
Stardust   29
Statues   11

T
Three Hours Past Midnight   50

Time	33
Time Passed	3, 30, 38, 53
Train Ride	55
Try Me	43

U
V

W
Walls	48
Wedding Dress	27
Willow Tree	24

X
Y
Z

About the Author

The Author was born in Chicago, Illinois, moving to Miami Beach, Washington, D.C. and other states before taking a hard landing in the Los Angeles area.

David started writing poems and other stories at an early age of nineteen and continued and off for many years putting them away. Most of them were hidden away in files and stored, as he moved around the country always looking for a home.

His life experiences are far too many to tell, going to many schools and having several jobs as he floated through his life. Since he was a young man, he had a compassion and yearning to write down the feelings that could not express verbally.

Music flowed and rhymes landed on paper of loves, fears, haunts, and life. This book of "Between Spirit & Substance" should, hopefully touch everyone.

The Author is currently working on a novel filled with adventure, intrigue, and suspense as well as a few more books on life and the constant ups, downs, and emotional challenges.

www.ingramcontent.com/pod-product-compliance
Lightning Source LLC
LaVergne TN
LVHW061601070526
838199LV00077B/7129